USBORNE
Big Picture
ATLAS

Emily Bone

ILLUSTRATED BY
Daniel Taylor

DESIGNED BY
Emily Barden

CONTENTS

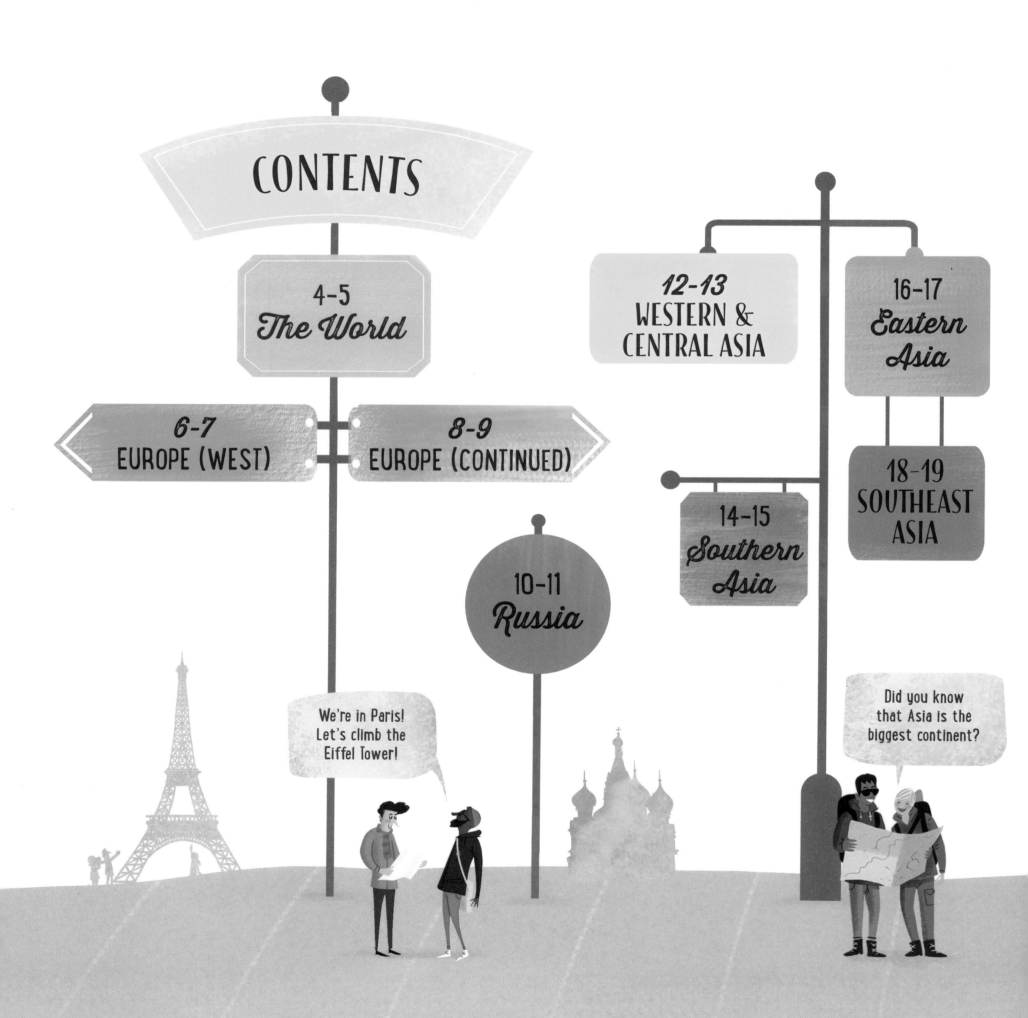

We're in Paris! Let's climb the Eiffel Tower!

Did you know that Asia is the biggest continent?

It's the Statue of Liberty! Where shall we go next?

Come on, let's explore!

THE WORLD

The world is divided up into seven large areas of land, called continents, and five oceans. This map of the world shows some of the things to look out for in this book.

Groups of people have lived in some areas for a very long time, and have a particular language and way of life. Inuit people live in northern Canada and Greenland.

The very top of the Earth is known as the North Pole.

The sea here is often frozen.

On maps, the Earth is divided up by imaginary lines. These are used to measure distances and find exactly where places are. The most important lines are the Equator, Tropics and Arctic and Antarctic Circles.

NORTH AMERICA

ATLANTIC OCEAN

EUROPE

TROPIC OF CANCER

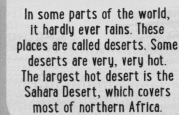

In some parts of the world, it hardly ever rains. These places are called deserts. Some deserts are very, very hot. The largest hot desert is the Sahara Desert, which covers most of northern Africa.

AFRICA

PACIFIC OCEAN

EQUATOR

The Equator is a line around the middle of the Earth. The hottest parts of the world are around the Equator. It rains here almost every day.

Between the Equator and the Tropics of Cancer and Capricorn it is very hot and often very wet.

SOUTH AMERICA

Huge forests, called rainforests, grow near the Equator. They're home to most of the world's plants and animals.

TROPIC OF CAPRICORN

Mountains are marked in purple on the maps like this. Most mountains are in groups called mountain ranges.

CANADA

OTTAWA

Boundaries between countries are marked with a line like this.

Each country has a main, capital, city or cities. These are marked with red dots.

SOUTHERN OCEAN

• WASHINGTON, D.C.

UNITED STATES OF AMERICA

Some countries are divided into smaller areas, such as states. Their boundary lines look like this.

The very bottom of the Earth is known as the South Pole. Many explorers have gone on expeditions to reach the Poles.

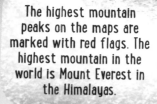

The highest mountain peaks on the maps are marked with red flags. The highest mountain in the world is Mount Everest in the Himalayas.

On each map, you'll see a globe, like this one. The area shown in the map is highlighted on the globe.

ARCTIC OCEAN

North of the Arctic Circle and south of the Antarctic Circle are the coldest places in the world.

ARCTIC CIRCLE

There are huge mountains and valleys under the sea too. The deepest point on Earth is the Mariana Trench, which is almost 11km (7 miles) deep.

ASIA

Most people in the world live in big cities. Shanghai in China has more people living there than any other city.

PACIFIC OCEAN

Rivers are shown as blue lines. The longest river in the world is the Nile, in Africa.

INDIAN OCEAN

AUSTRALASIA

The Great Barrier Reef is the world's largest structure. It can be seen from space.

Between the Equator and the Tropics are big areas of grassland, called savannas. Many animals, including giraffes, zebras and lions, roam on the grasslands in Africa.

Almost three-quarters of the Earth is covered by seas and oceans.

ANTARCTIC CIRCLE

ANTARCTICA

INTERNET LINKS

To find out more about maps and our fascinating world, go to www.usborne.com/quicklinks and type in the keywords 'big picture atlas'.

There are lots of amazing animals on the Earth. The blue whale is the biggest.

EUROPE (WEST)

Dog sledding is a speedy way to travel across a snowy landscape.

FINLAND

Lakeland canoeing

Mökki (summer house)

HELSINKI

Scandinavians have midsummer festivals to celebrate the longest day of the year.

Dala horse, a traditional painted wooden horse from Sweden

Baltic Sea

Reindeer

SWEDEN

At a midsummer festival, people dance around a decorated maypole.

STOCKHOLM

Little Mermaid statue, Copenhagen

Sami people are traditionally reindeer herders who live in the far north of Scandinavia.

Together, Norway, Sweden, Denmark and Finland are known as SCANDINAVIA.

Cross-country skiing

ARCTIC CIRCLE

Lake Vättern

Fika (a coffee break)

Lake Vänern

Glomma

NORWAY

Oslo Opera House

OSLO

Viking Ship Museum, Oslo

COPENHAGEN
DENMARK

Wurst sausage and pretzel bread

Moose

Norwegian Sea

Preikestolen (Pulpit Rock)

The Øresund Bridge links Sweden and Denmark.

Windmill

Old merchants' houses on the waterfront in Bergen

North Sea

The Lake District National Park

Icelandic fishing boat

Puffin colony

FAROE ISLANDS (DENMARK)

SHETLAND ISLANDS

ORKNEY ISLANDS

Edinburgh Castle, an historic fortress

Isle of Man TT motorcycle racing

White-tailed eagle

Pilot whale

ATLANTIC OCEAN

Cod

DUBLIN

IRELAND

ICELAND

At the Blue Lagoon, people bathe in a warm natural pool made blue by chemicals in the surrounding rocks.

• REYKJAVIK

Iceland is covered in volcanoes. Over 30 of them are active, which means they've erupted at least once in the last 10,000 years.

The Giant's Causeway is a rock formation in Northern Ireland. It was created millions of years ago by a volcanic eruption.

Irish folk musicians and dancer

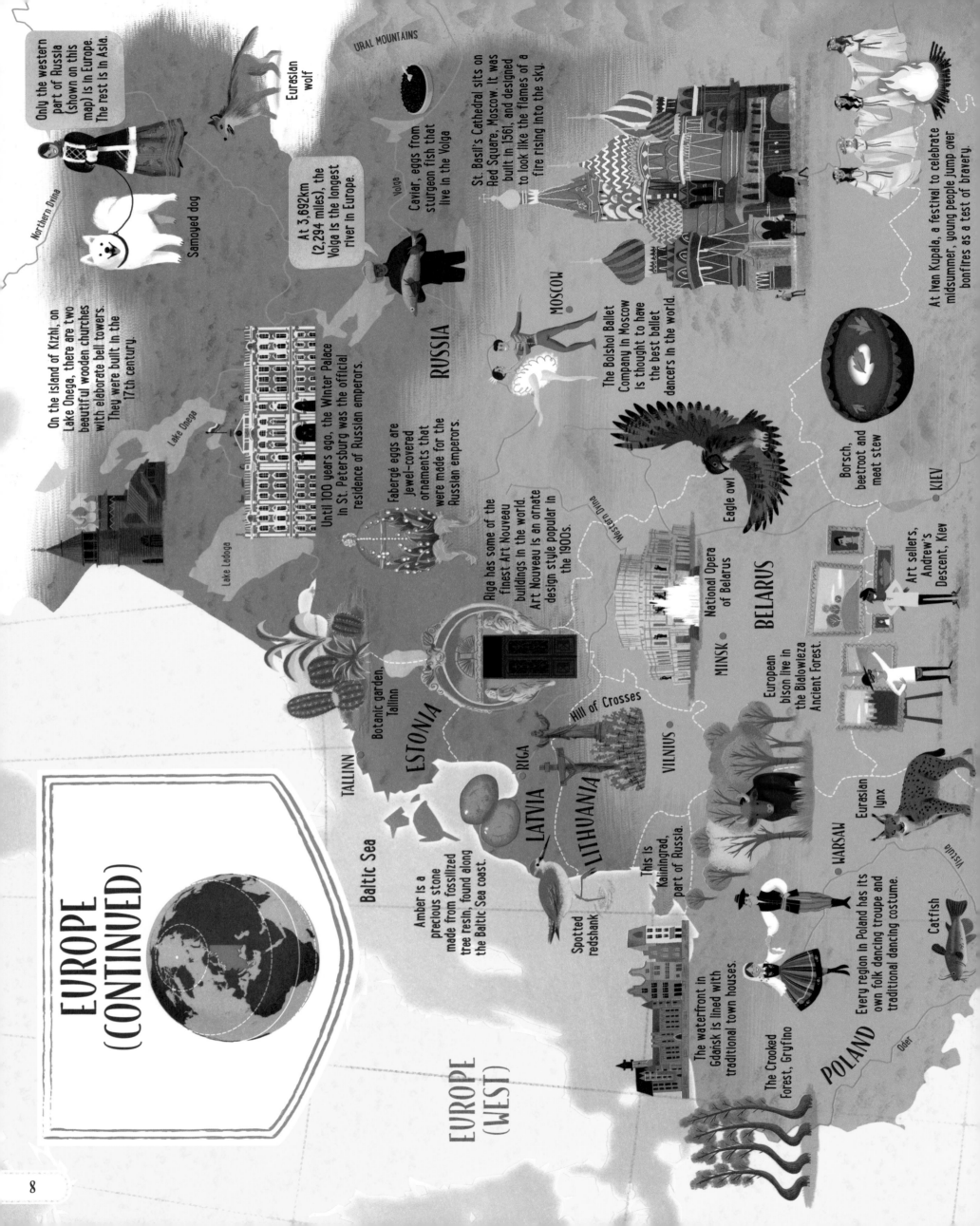

EUROPE (CONTINUED)

Only the western part of Russia (shown on this map) is in Europe. The rest is in Asia.

URAL MOUNTAINS

Eurasian wolf

Northern Dvina

Samoyed dog

Caviar, eggs from sturgeon fish that live in the Volga

Volga

At 3,692km (2,294 miles), the Volga is the longest river in Europe.

St. Basil's Cathedral sits on Red Square, Moscow. It was built in 1561, and designed to look like the flames of a fire rising into the sky.

At Ivan Kupala, a festival to celebrate midsummer, young people jump over bonfires as a test of bravery.

On the island of Kizhi, on Lake Onega, there are two beautiful wooden churches with elaborate bell towers. They were built in the 17th century.

Lake Onega

Lake Ladoga

Until 100 years ago, the Winter Palace in St. Petersburg was the official residence of Russian emperors.

Fabergé eggs are jewel-covered ornaments that were made for the Russian emperors.

MOSCOW

RUSSIA

The Bolshoi Ballet Company in Moscow is thought to have the best ballet dancers in the world.

Eagle owl

Borsch, beetroot and meat stew

KIEV

Riga has some of the finest Art Nouveau buildings in the world. Art Nouveau is an ornate design style popular in the 1900s.

Western Dvina

National Opera of Belarus

Art sellers, Andrew's Descent, Kiev

Botanic garden, Tallinn

Hill of Crosses

MINSK

BELARUS

European bison live in the Bialowieza Ancient Forest.

ESTONIA

TALLINN

Baltic Sea

Amber is a precious stone made from fossilized tree resin, found along the Baltic Sea coast.

LATVIA · RIGA

LITHUANIA

VILNIUS

Eurasian lynx

Spotted redshank

This is Kaliningrad, part of Russia.

WARSAW

Vistula

EUROPE (WEST)

The waterfront in Gdańsk is lined with traditional town houses.

The Crooked Forest, Gryfino

Every region in Poland has its own folk dancing troupe and traditional dancing costume.

POLAND

Odra

Catfish

UKRAINE

Dnieper

Sea of Azov

Ski resorts near the town of Sochi, Russia, have hosted many winter sports events, including the 2014 Winter Olympic and Paralympic Games.

Car ferry

Chufut-Kale cave city

Dniester

CHIȘINĂU

MOLDOVA

Triumphal Arch

Great white pelican

Black Sea

The Thracian Tomb of Kazanlak is decorated with wall paintings made 2,400 years ago.

Most of Turkey is in Asia, but its far western end is in Europe. Turn to page 12 to find out about Turkey in Asia.

CYPRUS

NICOSIA

Greece has over 6,000 islands in the Aegean Sea. Crete is the biggest.

Mediterranean Sea

Selimiye Mosque, Edirne

CARPATHIAN MOUNTAINS

BUCHAREST

In the Merry Cemetery, Săpânța, tombstones are decorated with art and poems.

Rock sculpture of Decebalus, an ancient king

Bran Castle was said to have inspired the book *Dracula* by Bram Stoker.

European bee eater

BULGARIA

TURKEY

Samariá Gorge, Crete

CRETE

ROMANIA

In Hungary, people paint eggs at Easter to give as gifts.

Danube

SOFIA

Millennium Cross

SKOPJE

MACEDONIA

Traditional dancing, called horos, is popular across Greece. Each region has its own dance.

MOUNT OLYMPUS

Aegean Sea

ATHENS

SLOVAKIA

BRATISLAVA

BUDAPEST

HUNGARY

Great egret

BELGRADE

SERBIA

SARAJEVO

BOSNIA AND HERZEGOVINA

DINARIC ALPS

MONTENEGRO

PODGORICA

KOSOVO

PRISTINA

ALBANIA

TIRANA

Poppy

GREECE

Gyros (grilled meat) in pitta bread

There are lots of statues and ruins of ancient temples and other buildings in Greece. Some were built over 3,000 years ago.

Thermal (hot) public baths, Budapest

Mehmed Paša Sokolović Bridge, Višegrad, a 500-year-old bridge

Adriatic Sea

The Parthenon is a famous ancient Greek temple in Athens. It was built for the goddess Athena.

RUSSIA

Russia is the world's biggest country, covering 11.5% of the Earth's land. It's in both Europe and Asia.

The sea here is frozen for most of the year.

ARCTIC OCEAN

The Northern Lights are a stunning natural light show that can be seen in the night sky within the Arctic Circle.

FRANZ JOSEF LAND

EUROPE (WEST)

The Millennium of Russia monument was built in Veliky Novgorod in 1862, to celebrate a thousand years of Russian history. It's covered with statues of Russian leaders.

Container ship

Barents Sea

NOVAYA ZEMLYA ISLAND

Polar bear

Gyrfalcon

Nenet people live in tents made from reindeer skins.

Kara Sea

Balalaika, a traditional Russian instrument

The Kremlin, in Moscow, is the official residence of the Russian Parliament. It's on Red Square, next to St. Basil's Cathedral (page 8).

Lake Ladoga

Lake Onega

The Nenet people are reindeer herders who live in northern Siberia.

Snowy owl

ARCTIC CIRCLE

Ob

Mountain hare

• MOSCOW

EUROPE   ASIA

Volga

Forests of silver birch trees cover large areas of eastern Russia.

Brown bear

Ushanka, a traditional Russian fur hat with ear flaps

In public baths called banyas bathers beat themselves with branches, as they believe it cures all kinds of illnesses.

Don

URAL MOUNTAINS

Siberia is a huge area of Russia east of the Ural Mountains. Siberia gets very cold in winter. Some parts have reached below -60°C (-76°F).

The Ural Mountains mark the boundary between two continents. To the west is Europe, to the east is Asia.

Cloudberries

Irtysh

Yenisey

MOUNT ELBRUS

Ural

There are many sunflower farms in this part of Russia. Sunflower seeds are a popular snack.

Volga

Oil rig

Blini (pancakes) with caviar

Ob

ALTAI MOUNTAINS

Caspian Sea

WESTERN & CENTRAL ASIA

Bowhead whale

WRANGEL ISLAND

Arctic fox

Pollock fish

East Siberian Sea

Musk ox

Icebreaker ships are made from strong metal to break up ice as they sail through it.

NEW SIBERIAN ISLANDS

SEVERNAYA ZEMLYA

Thick-billed murre

Siberian husky

Bering Sea

Laptev Sea

In parts of northern Siberia, the ground is frozen most of the year and hardly anything grows. This is known as tundra.

Siberian Ibex

Sea otter

Russian thistle plants detach from their roots when the ground is frozen, and get blown around by the wind.

KAMCHATKA PENINSULA

Koryakskaya volcano

Siberian dwarf hamster

Caribou

Sea of Okhotsk

VERKHOYANSK MOUNTAINS

The taiga is a huge pine forest that covers northern Siberia.

Mammoth skeleton in the Yakutsk Mammoth Museum

Sea lion

Crested auklet

Pelmeni are dumplings eaten everywhere in Russia. They're often served with sour cream.

Lena

Sable

Aldan

Prehistoric animals have been found preserved in the ice in Siberia.

SAKHALIN ISLAND

Amur

Fishing trawler

Mir diamond mine is a huge, open pit 525m (1,722ft) deep, and 1,200m (3,900ft) wide.

Angara

People can hike on trails around Lake Baikal.

This is a train on the Trans-Siberian route from Moscow to Vladivostok. It's the longest train route in the world.

Amur

Ammonite fossils

A 17th-century wooden fortress in the Museum of Wooden Architecture, near Irkutsk

Lake Baikal

Amur

Lake Baikal is the deepest lake on Earth. In winter, its surface freezes solid.

EASTERN ASIA

Roads are marked out for people to drive across Lake Baikal when it's frozen.

S-56 Second World War Submarine Museum, Vladivostok

Black Sea

Mediterranean Sea

Gate of Salutation, Topkapi Palace, Istanbul

Cave houses carved out of volcanic rock formations, Cappadocia

Gergeti Trinity Church in the Caucasus Mountains

ANKARA

Bathers having full-body wash at a hamam (Turkish bath)

TURKEY

TAURUS MOUNTAINS

CAUCASUS MOUNTAINS

GEORGIA

TBILISI

Ruins of ancient statues on Mount Nemrut

ARMENIA

YEREVAN

The Dome of the Rock, in Jerusalem, is an important religious site for Jewish and Muslim people.

NORTHERN AFRICA

ISRAEL

LEBANON

BEIRUT

SYRIA

DAMASCUS

Lake Van

This is part of Azerbaijan.

Tigris

Lake Urmia

AZERBAIJAN

BAKU

Palace of the Shirvanshahs, Baku

Figs come from fig trees, which grow in this region.

Caspian Sea

JERUSALEM

Palestine

AMMAN

JORDAN

IRAQ

Euphrates

Amadiya is a village and resort set on top of a mountain 1,400m (4,600ft) high.

Date palm

The Dead Sea is the lowest point on Earth. The water is extremely salty, which makes people float.

Camel spider

BAGHDAD

Falafel, balls of fried, mashed chickpeas

TEHRAN

Iran used to be known as Persia. Iranian craftsmen weave Persian carpets – thick, heavy textiles with elaborate designs.

Ruins of Petra in Jordan, an ancient city carved out of rock

An oud is a traditional instrument from western Asia.

Kuwait Towers

ZAGROS MOUNTAINS

IRAN

Persepolis is an ancient Persian city, now in ruins. This is a two-headed griffin statue there.

Mada'in Saleh, rock tombs built more than 1,000 years ago

Millions of Muslims travel to Mecca every year. It is the birthplace of the Prophet Muhammad.

KUWAIT

KUWAIT CITY

Prehistoric rock carvings, Jubba

Oil rig

At 828m (2,716.5ft) tall, Burj Khalifa, Dubai, is the world's tallest building.

RIYADH

MANAMA

BAHRAIN

QATAR

Red Sea

The Kaaba in Mecca is a sacred building in the middle of the Masjid al-Haram mosque.

DOHA

UNITED ARAB EMIRATES

SAUDI ARABIA

Souq (market)

Arabian oryx

ABU DHABI

Goat herders who live in the Zagros Mountains

SARAWAT MOUNTAINS

Hamadryas baboons

ARABIAN DESERT

Sand cat

Camel racing is a very popular sport here.

MUSCAT

Ghost crab

YEMEN

SANA'A

Buildings in old Sana'a

Fenugreek is grown for its leaves and seeds, which are used in cooking.

Frankincense, a perfumed tree resin (dried sap)

OMAN

Sultan Qaboos Grand Mosque, Muscat

TROPIC OF CANCER

Roses are grown in Oman to make rosewater.

Green turtles come onto the beaches of Oman to lay eggs.

Arabian Sea

RUSSIA

The Aral Sea used to be one of the biggest lakes in the world. It dried out, shrinking to just a tenth of its original size.

Khan Shatyr, in Astana, is a giant tent with a boating lake, beach resort, shopping and entertainment venues inside.

A Kazakh folk dance called Kara-Zhorga is performed at festivals. Dancers mimic the movements of horses.

There are many abandoned boats on the dry lake bed.

Aral Sea

ASTANA

Rockets launch into space from the Baikonur Cosmodrome, taking astronauts and supplies to the International Space Station.

Amu Darya

KAZAKHSTAN

Irtysh

National dress of Turkmenistan

The clay earth in Uzbekistan is used to make ornate ceramic objects.

Tomb of Kozha Akhmed Yasaui, an important 14th-century holy man

Taimen

Lake Balkhash

KARA KUM DESERT

Honey badger

ASHGABAT

TURKMENISTAN

UZBEKISTAN

TASHKENT

BISHKEK

KYRGYZSTAN

Apples grow wild all over Kazakhstan.

Argali sheep

Lake Issyk

Minaret of Jam

Pomegranates

DUSHANBE

TAJIKISTAN

TIEN SHAN MOUNTAINS

Afghan hound

HINDU KUSH MOUNTAINS

EASTERN ASIA

KABUL

AFGHANISTAN

Long-legged buzzard

This area is very mountainous. It's easiest to travel on the steep, rocky roads on horseback.

Persian leopard

SOUTHERN ASIA

WESTERN & CENTRAL ASIA

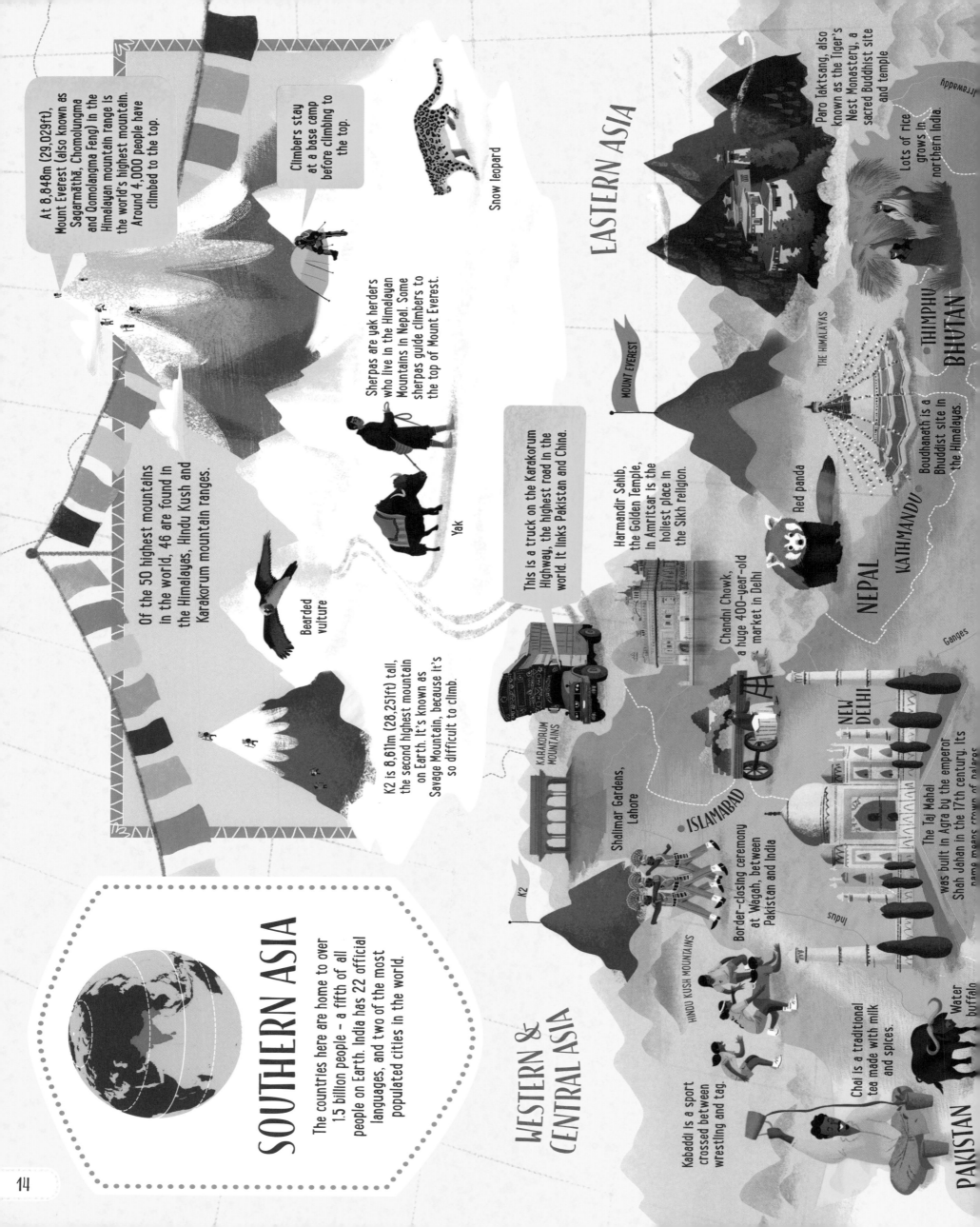

SOUTHERN ASIA

The countries here are home to over 1.5 billion people – a fifth of all people on Earth. India has 22 official languages, and two of the most populated cities in the world.

At 8,848m (29,029ft), Mount Everest (also known as Sagarmāthā, Chomolungma and Qomolangma Feng) in the Himalayan mountain range is the world's highest mountain. Around 4,000 people have climbed to the top.

Climbers stay at a base camp before climbing to the top.

Snow leopard

Of the 50 highest mountains in the world, 46 are found in the Himalayas, Hindu Kush and Karakorum mountain ranges.

Sherpas are yak herders who live in the Himalayan Mountains in Nepal. Some sherpas guide climbers to the top of Mount Everest.

Yak

Bearded vulture

K2 is 8,611m (28,251ft) tall, the second highest mountain on Earth. It's known as Savage Mountain, because it's so difficult to climb.

This is a truck on the Karakorum Highway, the highest road in the world. It links Pakistan and China.

Harmandir Sahib, the Golden Temple, in Amritsar is the holiest place in the Sikh religion.

Chandni Chowk, a huge 400-year-old market in Delhi

KARAKORUM MOUNTAINS

K2

Shalimar Gardens, Lahore

ISLAMABAD

Border-closing ceremony at Wagah, between Pakistan and India

NEW DELHI

The Taj Mahal was built in Agra by the emperor Shah Jahan in the 17th century. Its name means crown of palaces.

Indus

HINDU KUSH MOUNTAINS

Kabaddi is a sport crossed between wrestling and tag.

Chai is a traditional tea made with milk and spices.

Water buffalo

PAKISTAN

WESTERN & CENTRAL ASIA

EASTERN ASIA

Paro Taktsang, also known as the Tiger's Nest Monastery, a sacred Buddhist site and temple

Lots of rice grows in northern India.

Irrawaddy

MOUNT EVEREST

THE HIMALAYAS

THIMPHU

BHUTAN

Boudhanath is a Buddhist site in the Himalayas.

Red panda

KATHMANDU

NEPAL

Ganges

Sun bear

Painted rickshaw

BURMA (MYANMAR)

NAYPYIDAW

Bengal tiger

RANGOON

Shwedagon Zedi Daw, the Golden Pagoda, in Rangoon is a stupa – a Buddhist monument.

DHAKA

Bay of Bengal

ANDAMAN AND NICOBAR ISLANDS

Hammerhead shark

INDIAN OCEAN

Fishing boat

Brahminy kite, a type of sea eagle that eats fish

Indian rhinoceros

Lotus flowers grow from boggy ground. In Buddhism and Hinduism, they symbolize purity and rebirth.

Asian elephants are incredibly important in India. They are sacred to Hindus.

Tea is grown on rainy mountainsides in Sri Lanka. Each tea leaf is picked by hand, then dried.

Seaplane

EQUATOR

INDIA

At Holi festival people celebrate the coming of spring. They throw dyed powder to symbolize the blooming of spring flowers.

People who follow the Hindu religion bathe in the Ganges River as a form of worship.

Godavari

Charminar Mosque, Hyderabad

Yoga originated among Hindus and Buddhists in ancient India. It involves meditation, a way of focusing the body and mind.

SRI LANKA

Oranges

COLOMBO

SRI JAYAWARDENEPURA KOTTE

The Maldives is made up of around 1,200 islands in the Indian Ocean, but only 200 have people living on them.

Grouper

Rhesus macaques

Coconuts

Wild black pepper

MALÉ

Boduberu is a fast dance performed by 20 people and accompanied by drummers.

TROPIC OF CANCER

Curries can be served with roti, an Indian flatbread.

Arabian Sea

In India, many people wear traditional clothing.

Women wear long pieces of patterned cloth wrapped and tucked around them, called saris.

Men wear long tunics called kurta.

This man is wearing material wrapped around his legs, called a dhoti.

Scotch bonnet peppers are used in many Maldivian dishes.

Coral are small marine animals that live in warm, shallow seas. There are lots around the coasts of the Indian Ocean.

LAKSHADWEEP ISLANDS

MALDIVES

Curry, a spiced meat or vegetable stew

EASTERN ASIA

WESTERN & CENTRAL ASIA

RUSSIA

Wrestling is a popular sport in Mongolia. Competitors perform a dance at the beginning and end of each match.

Statue of Ghengis Khan, founder of the Mongol Empire

ULAN BATOR

MONGOLIA

Mogao Caves of the thousand Buddhas

TIEN SHAN MOUNTAINS

ALTAI MOUNTAINS

Przewalski's horse is a type of wild horse from Mongolia. Horses provide milk and meat and also carry people and things.

Ger, a portable Mongolian tent

Traditional Mongolian dress is called deel – embroidered silk robes worn with heavy silver and coral necklaces.

Jerboa

GOBI DESERT

Saxaul trees grow on sand dunes.

Ruddy shelduck

Id Kah Mosque

Chopsticks

Noodles are made from rolled, stretched dough. They're eaten in China and across eastern Asia.

Naked carp

Qinghai lake

Yellow

CHINA

KARAKORUM MOUNTAINS

KUNLUN MOUNTAINS

K2

Pangolins have bodies covered in thick scales. If they're attacked, they roll up to protect themselves.

Snub-nosed monkey

Yangtze

Bamboo

K2 mountain is on the border between China and Pakistan. It's the world's second highest mountain (see page 14).

Potala Palace, a 400-year-old palace and sacred site

Brahmaputra

Salween

THE HIMALAYAS

Giant pandas only eat bamboo, which grows in forests in China.

Western China is covered with mountains and deserts and there aren't any big towns or cities.

Over one and a quarter billion people live in China – more than any other country in the world.

The Leshan Giant Buddha is a stone statue carved out of a cliff face. It's 71m (233ft) tall.

TROPIC OF CANCER

SOUTHERN ASIA

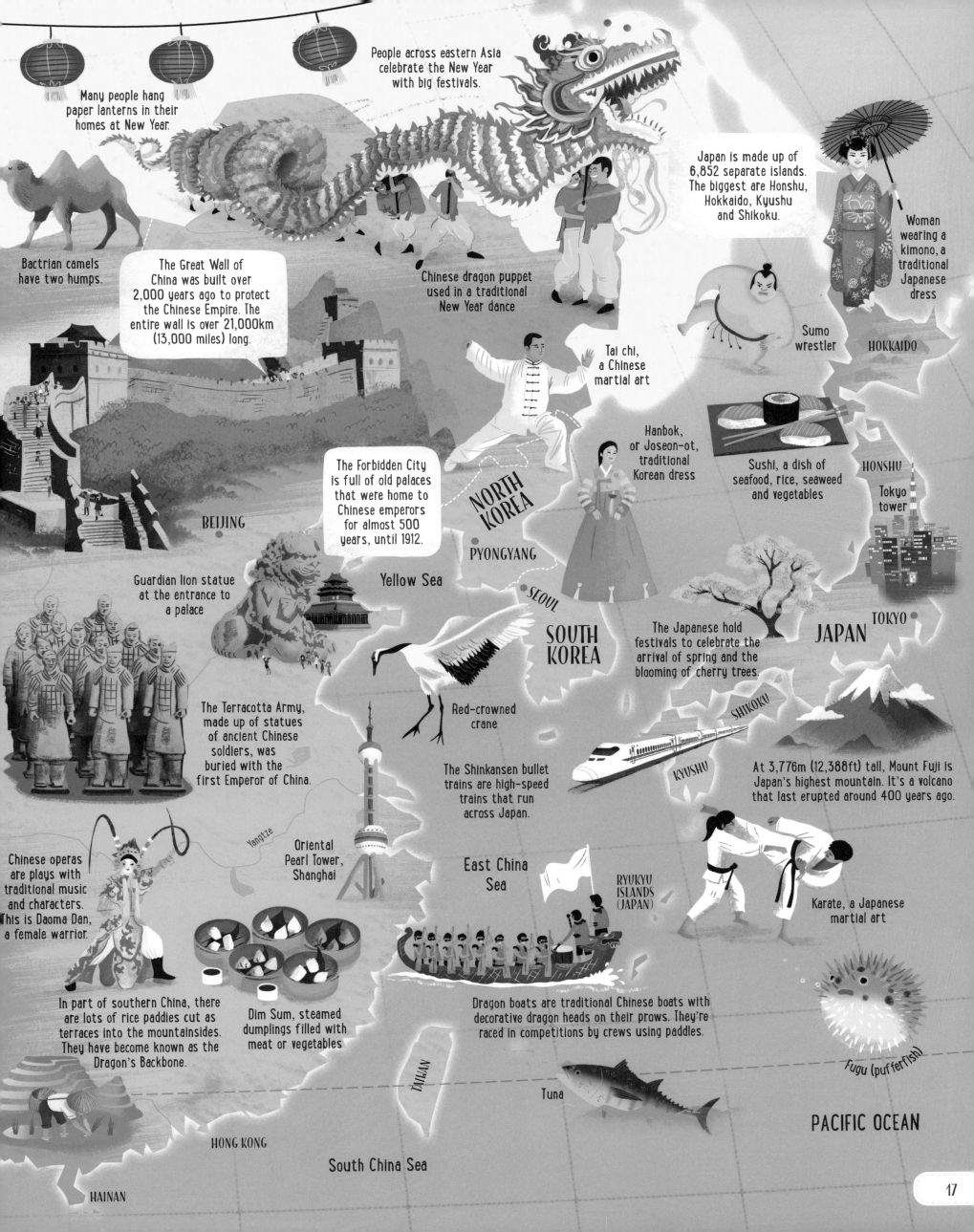

Many people hang paper lanterns in their homes at New Year.

People across eastern Asia celebrate the New Year with big festivals.

Japan is made up of 6,852 separate islands. The biggest are Honshu, Hokkaido, Kyushu and Shikoku.

Woman wearing a kimono, a traditional Japanese dress

Bactrian camels have two humps.

The Great Wall of China was built over 2,000 years ago to protect the Chinese Empire. The entire wall is over 21,000km (13,000 miles) long.

Chinese dragon puppet used in a traditional New Year dance

Sumo wrestler

HOKKAIDO

Tai chi, a Chinese martial art

Hanbok, or Joseon-ot, traditional Korean dress

Sushi, a dish of seafood, rice, seaweed and vegetables

HONSHU

Tokyo tower

The Forbidden City is full of old palaces that were home to Chinese emperors for almost 500 years, until 1912.

BEIJING

Guardian lion statue at the entrance to a palace

NORTH KOREA

PYONGYANG

Yellow Sea

SEOUL

SOUTH KOREA

The Japanese hold festivals to celebrate the arrival of spring and the blooming of cherry trees.

JAPAN

TOKYO

The Terracotta Army, made up of statues of ancient Chinese soldiers, was buried with the first Emperor of China.

Red-crowned crane

The Shinkansen bullet trains are high-speed trains that run across Japan.

SHIKOKU

KYUSHU

At 3,776m (12,388ft) tall, Mount Fuji is Japan's highest mountain. It's a volcano that last erupted around 400 years ago.

Chinese operas are plays with traditional music and characters. This is Daoma Dan, a female warrior.

Yangtze

Oriental Pearl Tower, Shanghai

East China Sea

RYUKYU ISLANDS (JAPAN)

Karate, a Japanese martial art

In part of southern China, there are lots of rice paddies cut as terraces into the mountainsides. They have become known as the Dragon's Backbone.

Dim Sum, steamed dumplings filled with meat or vegetables

Dragon boats are traditional Chinese boats with decorative dragon heads on their prows. They're raced in competitions by crews using paddles.

Fugu (pufferfish)

TAIWAN

Tuna

PACIFIC OCEAN

HONG KONG

South China Sea

HAINAN

EASTERN ASIA

Vat Phou are the ruins of a Hindu temple in southern Laos.

TROPIC OF CANCER

Nón lá are traditional cone-shaped hats, designed to keep the sun off the wearer's face and neck.

VIETNAM
HANOI

Hat seller

Junk boat, a traditional east-Asian boat

South China Sea

Pad Thai, a dish of fried noodles and spices

Mekong

LAOS
VIENTIANE

White-cheeked gibbon

South Sea mackerel

THAILAND

The Emerald Buddha, a small statue made from jade and gold

These are traditional Cambodian dancers performing a classical dance.

Kite surfing

Pygmy seahorses are tiny sea creatures that grow no more than 2cm (1in) long.

BANGKOK

CAMBODIA

The Grand Palace, Bangkok, is the residence of the King of Thailand.

PHNOM PENH

Bangka boat

Durian fruit is the smelliest fruit in the world.

Scorpion fish

Pho is a spiced Vietnamese noodle soup.

Barracuda

Atlas moths are the biggest flying bugs in the world.

Pitcher plants eat insects that fall into the plants' pitchers, or jugs, and can't get out.

Petronas Towers

Sumatran rhinoceros

BRUNEI
BANDAR SERI BEGAWAN

MALAYSIA

Sea snake

Slow loris

MALAYSIA

Southern Thailand, Malaysia and Indonesia are covered in tropical rainforests, filled with thousands of animals and plants.

KUALA LUMPUR
PUTRAJAYA

Lake Toba

SINGAPORE
SINGAPORE

INDONESIA

The island of Borneo is divided between three countries – Malaysia, Indonesia and Brunei.

Kapuas

Orangutans only live in the rainforests of Borneo and Sumatra.

INDONESIA

BORNEO

SUMATRA

Jungle trekking

At the cliff tombs in Toraja, people leave carved wooden figures, which they believe will protect the people buried there.

Rafflesia flowers grow on the floor of the Indonesian rainforest. They are the biggest flowers on Earth.

JAKARTA

INDIAN OCEAN

Borobudur Temple, the largest Buddhist temple in the world

JAVA

Reef shark

BALI

Gamelan drumming music is played on the islands of Java and Bali.

Bamboo shark

Philippine Sea

Philippine eagle

Triggerfish

SOUTHEAST ASIA

MANILA

Festivals are held to celebrate many different occasions in the Philippines. For the harvest festival in the region of Cebu, people dress up in grand outfits and dance in the streets.

Surfers come from around the world to surf the huge waves off the coasts of the Philippines.

PHILIPPINES

Wrasse

PACIFIC OCEAN

The bodies of pelagic jellyfish light up as they swim.

Tarsiers sleep during the day and wake at night. They have huge eyes to help them see in the dark.

Blue-ringed octopuses have skin that turns yellow with bright blue rings when they feel threatened.

Saltwater crocodile

Male birds of paradise have long, bright tails to attract females.

Sea slug

Epaulette shark

EQUATOR

Sweet potatoes

Coconut palms grow on islands across Indonesia.

INDONESIA

CELEBES

Indonesia is made up of over 18,000 islands, stretching from Sumatra to New Guinea.

Komodo dragons are the world's largest lizards. They can grow up to 3m (10ft) long, and their bite is poisonous.

Eagle ray

Dani people live in the rainforest on New Guinea island.

NEW GUINEA

AUSTRALASIA

DILI

EAST TIMOR

The shells of cowrie sea snails are used to make decorative necklaces.

Arafura Sea

ATLANTIC OCEAN

Mediterranean Sea

Zellige is a style of Moroccan patterned tile made from enamel and plaster.

The Rock in the Clouds on the Canary Islands was created by a volcanic eruption over four million years ago.

MADEIRA (PORTUGAL)

Street performers, such as snake charmers, entertain crowds in the Jemaa el-Fnaa square in Marrakesh.

RABAT

MOROCCO

ATLAS MOUNTAINS

ALGIERS

TUNIS

Tagine, meat and vegetable stew cooked in a cone-shaped pot

Merchants sell many spices. They're used a lot in cooking here.

TUNISIA

ALGERIA

TRIPOLI

A pirogue is a traditional canoe used for sailing at sea.

CANARY ISLANDS (SPAIN)

LAÂYOUNE

Snake charmer

Berber people are traditionally sheep herders who live in camps in the desert.

Mint tea with sugar is served after a meal.

Red Castle, Tripoli, an old fortress made from red sandstone

WESTERN SAHARA

Griffon vulture

Camels can go for days without food and water. They carry people and goods across the desert.

Sahara means 'Great Desert' in Arabic, and the Sahara is the largest hot desert in the world. It covers most of northern Africa.

Deathstalker scorpion

Fennec foxes live in burrows during the day, then come out at night when it's cooler.

MAURITANIA

The Dogon people of Mali perform dances for different ceremonies wearing masks and stilts.

The Great Mosque of Djenné is built from bricks of sand and earth.

SAHARA DESERT

Giraffes are the tallest animals in the world. They can grow more than 5m (18ft) tall, and eat leaves from the tops of trees.

NOUAKCHOTT

SENEGAL

Nile perch can grow up to 2m (6½ft) long.

MALI

NIGER

NIAMEY

Niger

N'DJA

THE GAMBIA

DAKAR

BAMAKO

BURKINA FASO

OUAGADOUGOU

BANJUL

Nigeria has a distinctive national dress. Women wear large, patterned headscarves, called geles.

BISSAU

GUINEA-BISSAU

GUINEA

Chimpanzee

White Volta

BENIN

CONAKRY

Warthog, a type of wild African pig

TOGO

PORTO-NOVO

Benué

FREETOWN

Presidential Palace in Yaoundé with the Cameroonian flag

SIERRA LEONE

LIBERIA

YAMOUSSOUKRO

GHANA

LOME

NIGERIA

ABUJA

MONROVIA

Pygmy hippopotamus

IVORY COAST

ACCRA

Jollof is a Nigerian dish of rice with tomatoes and spices. It's often served with fried chicken and plantain.

MALABO

YAOUNDÉ

CAMEROON

CAPE VERDE

Elmina castle is a 700-year-old trading post. It's the oldest building in this part of Africa.

EQUATORIAL GUINEA

Cape Verde is made up of a group of islands in the Atlantic Ocean, off the west coast of northern Africa.

Fishermen catch Cape rock lobsters using hoop nets.

Humpback dolphins have small humps on their backs.

PRAIA

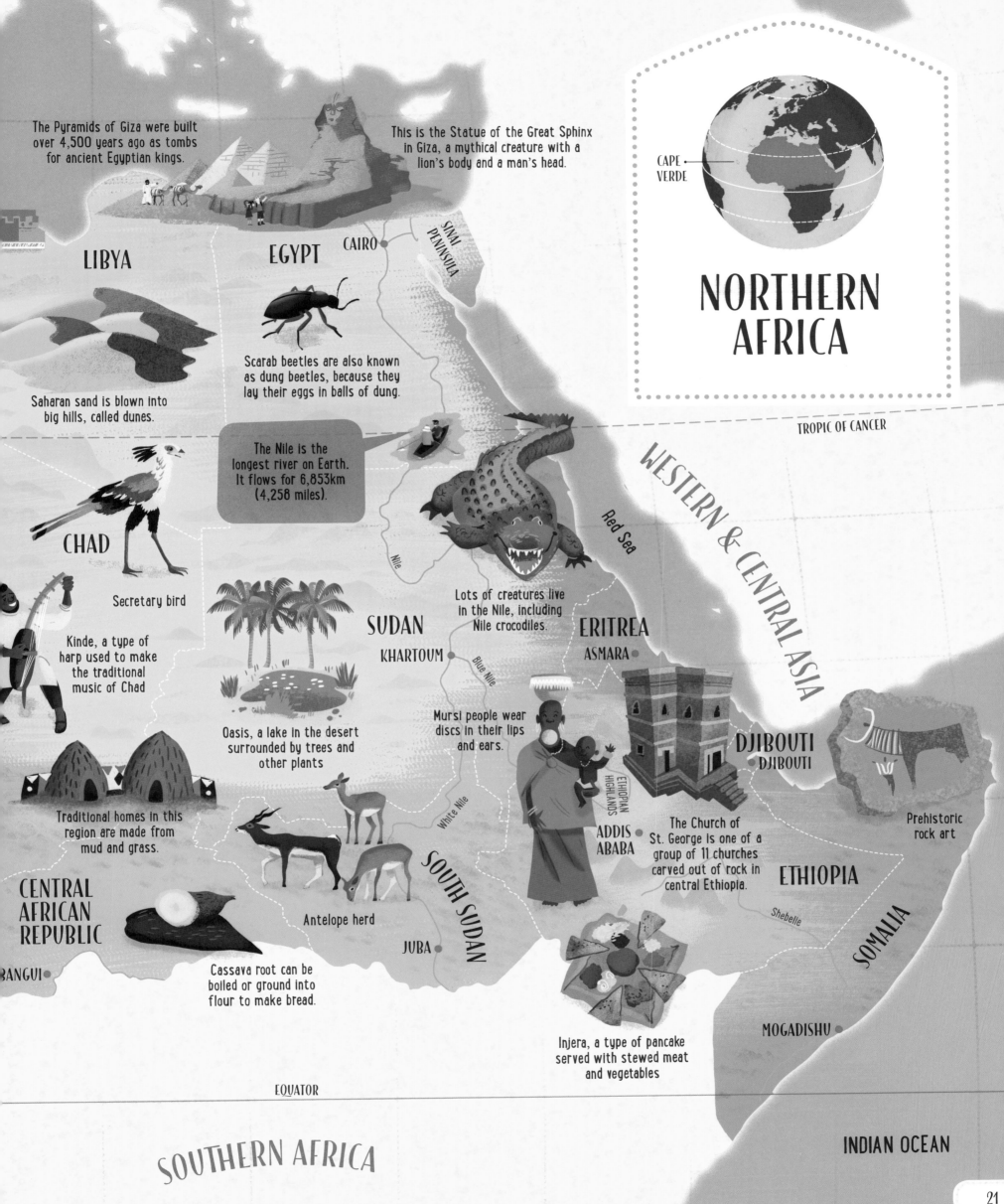

The Pyramids of Giza were built over 4,500 years ago as tombs for ancient Egyptian kings.

This is the Statue of the Great Sphinx in Giza, a mythical creature with a lion's body and a man's head.

CAPE VERDE

LIBYA

EGYPT

CAIRO

SINAI PENINSULA

Saharan sand is blown into big hills, called dunes.

Scarab beetles are also known as dung beetles, because they lay their eggs in balls of dung.

TROPIC OF CANCER

The Nile is the longest river on Earth. It flows for 6,853km (4,258 miles).

WESTERN & CENTRAL ASIA

Red Sea

CHAD

Secretary bird

Nile

Lots of creatures live in the Nile, including Nile crocodiles.

ERITREA

ASMARA

Kinde, a type of harp used to make the traditional music of Chad

SUDAN

KHARTOUM

Blue Nile

DJIBOUTI
DJIBOUTI

Mursi people wear discs in their lips and ears.

ETHIOPIAN HIGHLANDS

Prehistoric rock art

Oasis, a lake in the desert surrounded by trees and other plants

White Nile

ADDIS ABABA

The Church of St. George is one of a group of 11 churches carved out of rock in central Ethiopia.

ETHIOPIA

Traditional homes in this region are made from mud and grass.

Shebelle

CENTRAL AFRICAN REPUBLIC

Antelope herd

SOUTH SUDAN

JUBA

SOMALIA

BANGUI

Cassava root can be boiled or ground into flour to make bread.

MOGADISHU

Injera, a type of pancake served with stewed meat and vegetables

EQUATOR

SOUTHERN AFRICA

INDIAN OCEAN

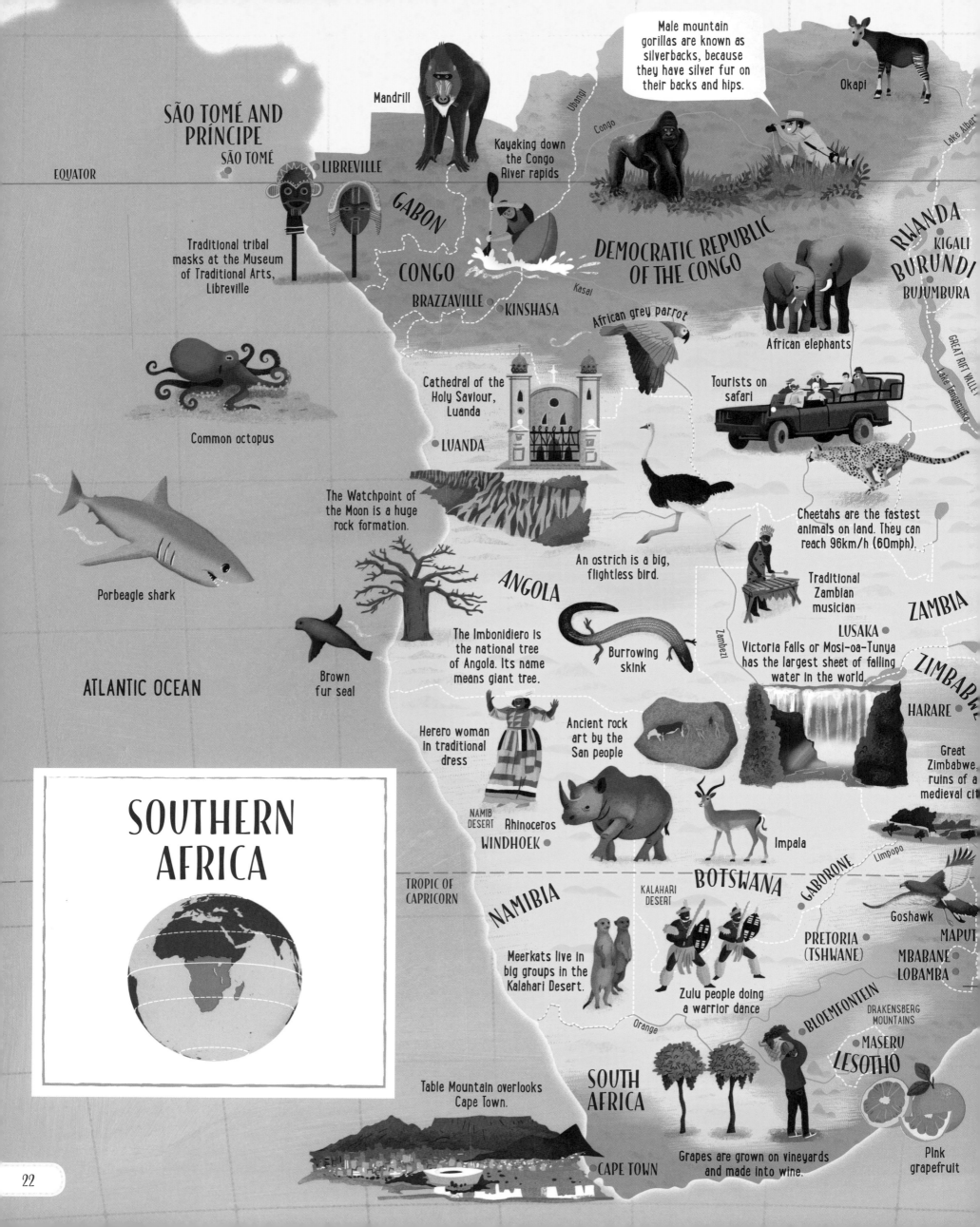

Male mountain gorillas are known as silverbacks, because they have silver fur on their backs and hips.

Okapi

Mandrill

SÃO TOMÉ AND PRÍNCIPE
SÃO TOMÉ

EQUATOR

LIBREVILLE

Kayaking down the Congo River rapids

DEMOCRATIC REPUBLIC OF THE CONGO

Ubangi

Congo

RWANDA
KIGALI
BURUNDI
BUJUMBURA

Lake Albert

GABON

Traditional tribal masks at the Museum of Traditional Arts, Libreville

CONGO
BRAZZAVILLE   KINSHASA

Kasai

African grey parrot

African elephants

GREAT RIFT VALLEY

Lake Tanganyika

Common octopus

Cathedral of the Holy Saviour, Luanda

LUANDA

Tourists on safari

Porbeagle shark

The Watchpoint of the Moon is a huge rock formation.

An ostrich is a big, flightless bird.

ANGOLA

Cheetahs are the fastest animals on land. They can reach 96km/h (60mph).

Traditional Zambian musician

ZAMBIA

Brown fur seal

The Imbondiero is the national tree of Angola. Its name means giant tree.

Burrowing skink

Zambezi

LUSAKA

Victoria Falls or Mosi-oa-Tunya has the largest sheet of falling water in the world.

ZIMBABWE

ATLANTIC OCEAN

Herero woman in traditional dress

Ancient rock art by the San people

HARARE

Great Zimbabwe, ruins of a medieval city

NAMIB DESERT   Rhinoceros

WINDHOEK

Impala

SOUTHERN AFRICA

TROPIC OF CAPRICORN

NAMIBIA

KALAHARI DESERT

BOTSWANA

GABORONE

Limpopo

Goshawk

MAPUTO

Meerkats live in big groups in the Kalahari Desert.

Zulu people doing a warrior dance

PRETORIA (TSHWANE)

MBABANE
LOBAMBA

BLOEMFONTEIN   DRAKENSBERG MOUNTAINS

Orange

MASERU
LESOTHO

Table Mountain overlooks Cape Town.

SOUTH AFRICA

Grapes are grown on vineyards and made into wine.

Pink grapefruit

CAPE TOWN

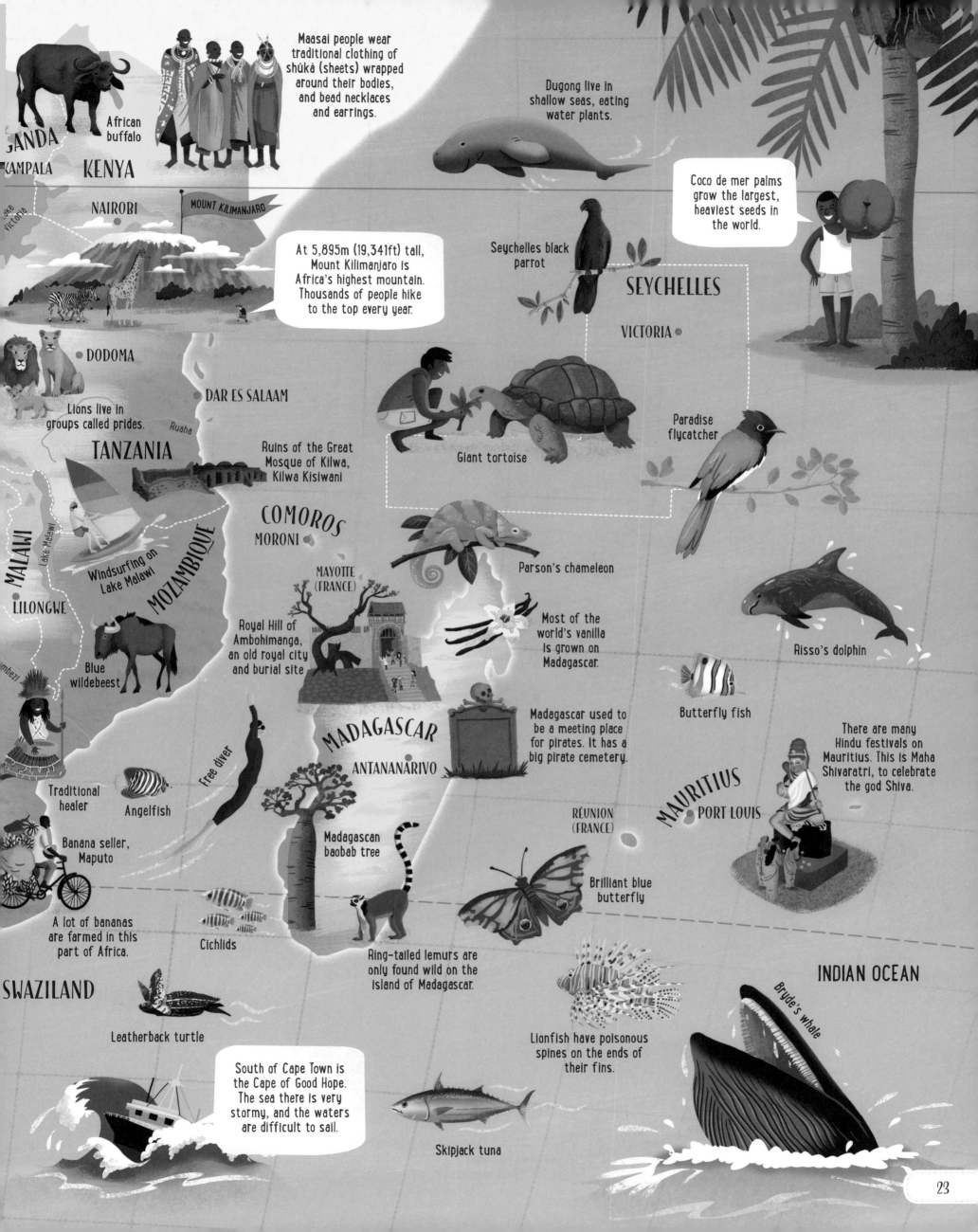

UGANDA

KAMPALA

KENYA

African buffalo

NAIROBI

Maasai people wear traditional clothing of shúkà (sheets) wrapped around their bodies, and bead necklaces and earrings.

Dugong live in shallow seas, eating water plants.

Coco de mer palms grow the largest, heaviest seeds in the world.

MOUNT KILIMANJARO

At 5,895m (19,341ft) tall, Mount Kilimanjaro is Africa's highest mountain. Thousands of people hike to the top every year.

Seychelles black parrot

SEYCHELLES

VICTORIA

DODOMA

Lions live in groups called prides.

DAR ES SALAAM

Ruaha

Giant tortoise

Paradise flycatcher

TANZANIA

Ruins of the Great Mosque of Kilwa, Kilwa Kisiwani

COMOROS

MOZAMBIQUE

MALAWI

MORONI

Parson's chameleon

Windsurfing on Lake Malawi

MAYOTTE (FRANCE)

LILONGWE

Royal Hill of Ambohimanga, an old royal city and burial site

Most of the world's vanilla is grown on Madagascar.

Risso's dolphin

Blue wildebeest

Butterfly fish

Free diver

MADAGASCAR

Madagascar used to be a meeting place for pirates. It has a big pirate cemetery.

There are many Hindu festivals on Mauritius. This is Maha Shivaratri, to celebrate the god Shiva.

ANTANANARIVO

Traditional healer

Angelfish

RÉUNION (FRANCE)

MAURITIUS

PORT LOUIS

Banana seller, Maputo

Madagascan baobab tree

Brilliant blue butterfly

A lot of bananas are farmed in this part of Africa.

Cichlids

SWAZILAND

Ring-tailed lemurs are only found wild on the island of Madagascar.

INDIAN OCEAN

Bryde's whale

Leatherback turtle

Lionfish have poisonous spines on the ends of their fins.

South of Cape Town is the Cape of Good Hope. The sea there is very stormy, and the waters are difficult to sail.

Skipjack tuna

The Iditarod is a dog sled race from Anchorage to Nome, over 1,600km (1,000 miles) long. The race can last up to 15 days.

USA | CANADA

ALASKA is a state of the USA.

Canadian timber wolves

Humpback whale

Yukon

DENALI

Denali (also known as Mount McKinley) is the highest mountain in North America. It's 6,190m (20,310ft) high.

Sockeye salmon swim from the Yukon River into the Pacific Ocean and back to lay eggs.

Ice fishing

ARCTIC CIRCLE

Great Bear Lake

Grizzly bears hunt salmon from rivers.

NORTHWEST TERRITORIES

Great Slave Lake

YUKON

Mackenzie

PACIFIC OCEAN

Killer whale

Walruses

Cruise liner

The First Nations Totem Pole in Vancouver celebrates native peoples living in Canada.

Peace

Banff National Park is Canada's oldest national park. Mountain bikers ride on trails through the mountains.

USA & CANADA

Canada and the United States of America are divided up into separate regions called states, provinces or territories. The USA has 50 states. Canada has ten provinces and three territories.

HAWAII

Giant redwoods are the tallest trees on Earth. One redwood, General Sherman, is the tallest, at 84m (275ft).

BRITISH COLUMBIA

Fraser

Lumberjack

ALBERTA

ROCKY MOUNTAINS

Columbia

American bison

WASHINGTON

OREGON

IDAHO

Snake

The flag of the USA has 50 stars, one for each state.

HAWAII

Hawaii is the USA's 50th state. It's a group of islands in the Pacific Ocean.

Ukulele

KAUAI

Hula dancing

O'AHU

MOLOKA'I

MAUI

Surfing

HAWAII

Golden Gate Bridge, San Francisco

CALIFORNIA

Las Vegas casinos

UTAH

GREAT BASIN DESERT

NEVADA

MOJAVE DESERT

HOLLYWOOD

Hibiscus flowers

Kilauea volcano, the most active volcano on Earth

PACIFIC OCEAN

Many movies are made at the Hollywood Studios, Los Angeles.

Saguaro are huge cactus plants that grow in the Sonoran Desert.

SONO DES

ARI

Colo

Common dolphin

Polar bear and cubs

BAFFIN ISLAND

Snowy owl

The Canadian Mounted Police are the national police force of Canada.

The Canadian flag is called the Maple Leaf. Canada has huge maple forests, and the leaf is Canada's national symbol.

NUNAVUT

Oil rig

Beluga whale

The Inuit people live in parts of north-eastern Canada.

Maple syrup is made from the sugary sap of maple trees.

Labrador dog

NEWFOUNDLAND & LABRADOR

Hudson Bay

Canada's national dish is poutine, fries topped with cheese curd and gravy.

PRINCE EDWARD ISLAND

ATLANTIC OCEAN

Ice hockey players

MANITOBA

Canada geese

CN Tower, Toronto

QUEBEC

MAINE

NEW BRUNSWICK

NOVA SCOTIA

Lobster roll

SKATCHEWAN

ONTARIO

These are the five Great Lakes. They make up the biggest group of lakes in the world.

St. Lawrence

APPALACHIAN MOUNTAINS

Lake Winnipeg

CANADA

USA

OTTAWA

NEW HAMPSHIRE

VERMONT

Saskatchewan

Lake Manitoba

Lake Superior

NEW YORK

MASSACHUSETTS

Cowboy

MINNESOTA

MICHIGAN

Lake Huron

Lake Ontario

RHODE ISLAND

CONNECTICUT

NORTH DAKOTA

The bald eagle is the national symbol of the USA.

WISCONSIN

Lake Michigan

Baseball player

Lake Erie

Niagara Falls

NEW JERSEY

PENNSYLVANIA

The Statue of Liberty, New York City

Missouri

MONTANA

Tornado

This area is covered with corn and wheat farms.

IOWA

ILLINOIS

Illinois

INDIANA

Ohio

OHIO

WASHINGTON, D.C.

DELAWARE

MARYLAND

WYOMING

SOUTH DAKOTA

Old Faithful, a geyser in Yellowstone National Park

NEBRASKA

MISSOURI

Indianapolis 500 motor racing

KENTUCKY

WEST VIRGINIA

VIRGINIA

NORTH CAROLINA

Wild turkey

The White House in Washington, D.C., is the home of the US President.

COLORADO

Arkansas

KANSAS

TENNESSEE

Country music singer, Nashville

SOUTH CAROLINA

GEORGIA

Kennedy Space Center, now a museum where rockets used to fly into space

Great White shark

The Grand Canyon is a huge canyon in Arizona. It's over 5km (1 mile) deep.

NEW MEXICO

OKLAHOMA

Alligator

ARKANSAS

Mississippi

MISSISSIPPI

ALABAMA

FLORIDA

The southeast of the USA is frequently hit by hurricanes – huge storms with very strong winds.

CHIHUAHUAN DESERT

Red

Steamboat

Because so many peaches grow in Georgia, it's known as the Peach State.

Gulf of Mexico

Longhorn cattle

TEXAS

LOUISIANA

Many cities in the USA have their own American football teams.

Rio Grande

Hopi people live in Arizona. Young Hopi perform a dance called the Butterfly Dance.

Mexican free-tailed bats fly from the USA to Mexico and back each year.

Manatees live in the warm, shallow seas of the Gulf of Mexico.

CENTRAL AMERICA & THE CARIBBEAN

25

Mexican wrestling is known as *Lucha Libre*. Wrestlers dress up in bold costumes, including masks and capes.

SONORAN DESERT

Mexican redknee tarantula

Mariachi is traditional Mexican music with singing accompanied by fast-paced guitars and violins.

Fruit from prickly pear cactus plants is used in Mexican cooking.

CHIHUAHUAN DESERT

Río Grande

SIERRA MADRE OCCIDENTAL

BAJA CALIFORNIA

There are lots of oyster farms in the Gulf of Mexico, and oysters are a popular meal here.

Cougar

Conchos

Spicy peppers grow under the hot Mexican sun.

Mexican street food is made to be eaten while walking along. This is a burrito – a tortilla (flatbread) stuffed with meat and beans.

SIERRA MADRE ORIENTAL

Marlin

Dahlias are Mexico's national flowers.

TROPIC OF CANCER

Red snapper

Gulf of Mexico

The Mayan people have lived in Mexico and Central America for over 4,000 years

Body boarder

MEXICO

Statue of the Aztec sun goddess Chalchiuhtlicue

Pyramid at Chichen Itza, an ancient Mayan city

Aztec people ruled this region until the 16th century.

MEXICO CITY •

A condor is a type of vulture. It soars over mountains looking for carrion (dead meat).

Palace of Fine Arts, Mexico City

PACIFIC OCEAN

Aloe vera

Armadillo

Usumacinta

BELIZE
• BELMOPAN

Whale shark

China poblana is a traditional Mexican costume, worn for carnivals.

The Day of the Dead is a festival to remember family members who have died. Painted sugar skulls are left at people's graves.

GUATEMALA

GUATEMALA CITY

HONDURAS

TEGUCIGALPA

SAN SALVADOR

CENTRAL AMERICA & THE CARIBBEAN

There are many different types of whales in this part of the Atlantic Ocean. People go on boat tours to spot them.

EL SALVADOR

Toucans live in the rainforest in Nicaragua.

Fin whale

USA & CANADA

There are over 7,000 islands in the Caribbean Sea. When European explorers first discovered this area, they named it the West Indies, because it lies west of the Indies (their name for Asia).

Caribbean cruise liner

St. Lucia parrots are the only parrots that live on the island of St. Lucia.

Fishermen throw nets into the sea to catch fish.

Mahi mahi

ATLANTIC OCEAN

A conch is a sea creature with a large, ornate shell.

People go snorkelling to study underwater creatures.

There are carnivals on many Caribbean islands. This is the Sugar Mas Carnival which takes place on St. Kitts and Nevis every December.

Havana's old town is famous for vintage American cars from the 1950s.

NASSAU

THE BAHAMAS

Gardenia flower

Palm trees

ST. KITTS AND NEVIS

HAVANA

CUBA

TURKS AND CAICOS ISLANDS (UK)

DOMINICAN REPUBLIC

VIRGIN ISLANDS (UK)

ANGUILLA (UK)

ANTIGUA AND BARBUDA

ST. JOHN'S

BASSETERRE

GUADELOUPE (FRANCE)

Bee hummingbird

CAYMAN ISLANDS (UK)

HAITI

PORT-AU-PRINCE

SANTO DOMINGO

PUERTO RICO (USA)

VIRGIN ISLANDS (USA)

DOMINICA

ROSEAU

BARBADOS

Atole, a hot soup with cinnamon

Mambo is a quick, swaying dance that originated in Cuba.

JAMAICA

KINGSTON

MARTINIQUE (FRANCE)

ST. LUCIA

CASTRIES

ST. VINCENT AND THE GRENADINES

KINGSTOWN

BRIDGETOWN

Bananas grow in the warm, humid climate here. They're shipped to countries around the world.

Caribbean Sea

Reggae is a style of music that started in Jamaica.

Hawksbill sea turtle

CURAÇAO (THE NETHERLANDS)

BONAIRE (THE NETHERLANDS)

GRENADA

ST. GEORGE'S

Spider monkey

ARUBA (THE NETHERLANDS)

TRINIDAD AND TOBAGO

PORT-OF-SPAIN

NICARAGUA

MANAGUA

Container ship on the Panama Canal

The Panama Canal is a man-made waterway that links the Atlantic and the Pacific Oceans.

Cricket is popular across the Caribbean, where many islands have their own teams.

Scarlet ibis, the national bird of Trinidad and Tobago

COSTA RICA

SAN JOSÉ

Panama Canal

PANAMA CITY

PANAMA

Ocelots, also known as dwarf leopards, are wild cats that live across Central America.

SOUTH AMERICA

Two-toed sloths slowly climb through rainforest trees.

CENTRAL AMERICA
& THE CARIBBEAN

SOUTH AMERICA

GALÁPAGOS
ISLANDS

EASTER ISLAND

Joropo is a fast, swirling dance performed by couples. It's Venezuela's national dance.

Coffee beans are grown across South America.

Angel Falls is the world's highest waterfall. It's 979m (3,212ft) high.

Manta rays are huge fish that use 'wings' to swim through the sea. They can grow up to 9m (30ft) wide.

Tiger shark

Scarlet macaws

Sap from rubber trees is traditionally used to make rubber.

Capoeira is a Brazilian martial art that combines dance, acrobatics and music.

Sugar cane

Statue of Christ the Redeemer in Rio de Janeiro

Chocolate is made from beans inside cocoa pods, which grow on cacao trees.

Feijoada, a dish of black beans and stewed meat. It's Brazil's national dish.

São Francisco

• BRASÍLIA

BRAZIL

Tocantins

Cathedral of Brasília

Howler monkeys

Capybaras

Paraguay

Amazon river dolphin

Leafcutter ants

Piranha fish

Amazon

Tapajós

FRENCH GUIANA (FRANCE)

CAYENNE

SURINAME

PARAMARIBO

GUYANA

GEORGETOWN

Giant river otter

Brazilian wandering spider

Huaorani man

Kayapo man

Huaorani woman

The dark green area on this map is the Amazon Rainforest, the biggest tropical rainforest in the world. It's home to over a million species of plants, animals, birds, fish and insects, and over 400 different tribes of people.

Orchids grow on rainforest trees.

On Lake Titicaca, the Uru people live on more than 40 floating, man-made reed islands.

BOLIVIA

La Paz

Guinea pig

VENEZUELA

CARACAS

Orinoco

poison dart frog

Ticuna man

Jaguar

COLOMBIA

• BOGOTÁ

Magdalena

Boa constrictor

Cock of the rock, Peru's national bird

Quechua people live in the Andes Mountains in Peru.

Ucayali

San Francisco Church, Lima

• LIMA

PERU

ECUADOR

• QUITO

Harpy eagle

Spectacled bear cubs climb trees to escape from danger.

28

These are the remains of Machu Picchu, an ancient city built over 600 years ago by the Inca people.

Rio Carnival is a festival and samba dancing competition that fills the streets of Rio de Janeiro every year.

ATLANTIC OCEAN

Right whale

Cape Polonio lighthouse

Albatrosses have the largest wingspan of any bird – over 3m (9ft) wide.

SOUTH GEORGIA (UK)

Racing yacht

Sailors take part in round-the-world yacht races that pass through Cape Horn. The sea is very stormy, making it a challenge to sail here.

Empanadas are pies filled with meat or cheese.

Paraná

Pampas grass

URUGUAY

MONTEVIDEO

Tango is a dance that originated in Argentina. Dancers perform in the old town squares of Buenos Aires.

Elephant seal

Rockhopper penguins

PARAGUAY

ASUNCIÓN

Llama herd

BUENOS AIRES

Gaucho (Argentinian cowboy) with a lasso (a loop of rope that's thrown to catch cattle)

Darwin's rhea

Colorado

Magellanic penguins

Firecrown hummingbird

FALKLAND ISLANDS (UK)

TIERRA DEL FUEGO

CAPE HORN

Pilcomayo

Radio telescopes have been built in the Atacama Desert to detect distant stars and planets.

ARGENTINA

Quinoa

Monkey puzzle tree

Beach strawberry

Ceviche, fish or seafood in lime juice and spices

Red scorpion

ACONCAGUA

CHILE

ANDES MOUNTAINS

Perito Moreno glacier

LA PAZ

SUCRE

Viscacha

ATACAMA DESERT

SANTIAGO

PACIFIC OCEAN

The Andes Mountains stretch for over 7,242km (4,500 miles), making them the longest mountain range on Earth.

ANDES MOUNTAINS

Machu Picchu

Hand of the Desert, a sand sculpture

The Atacama Desert is the driest place on Earth. It can go for years without raining.

Galápagos giant tortoise

The Galápagos Islands are known for their wildlife. There are many species here that aren't found anywhere else in the world.

TROPIC OF CAPRICORN

ISLANDS OF SOUTH AMERICA

GALÁPAGOS ISLANDS (ECUADOR)

Blue-footed boobies

EASTER ISLAND (RAPA NUI) (CHILE)

Over 800 giant statues, known as Moai, were built on Easter Island by the Rapa Nui people around 700 years ago.

29

AUSTRALASIA

Australia is a massive island. It is divided up into six states.

Australasia is made up of Australia, New Zealand and Papua New Guinea.

Coral

TROPIC OF CAPRICORN

PACIFIC OCEAN

Surgeonfish

Crown-of-thorns starfish

Māori are native people of New Zealand. Māori men perform a traditional war dance called a haka.

WELLINGTON

Kiwis are flightless birds. They're the national bird of New Zealand.

Sheep

NEW ZEALAND

Weta, a giant bug similar to a grasshopper

Coral Sea

Cone snail

Giant clam

Yellow damselfish

Tasman Sea

The Great Barrier Reef is a huge underwater structure. It's made out of sea creatures called coral and is home to more than 1,500 species of fish.

Sydney Opera House

The Goroka Show is held every year. People across Papua New Guinea perform dances for the show.

PORT MORESBY

Lamington cake

Koala

CANBERRA
AUSTRALIAN CAPITAL TERRITORY

TASMANIA

Tree kangaroo

GREAT DIVIDING RANGE

Platypus

PAPUA NEW GUINEA

NEW GUINEA

GREAT BARRIER REEF

Mitchell

Copperhead snake

QUEENSLAND

Funnel web spider

Darling

NEW SOUTH WALES

Murray

Black swan

VICTORIA

The Tasmanian devil only lives on the Island of Tasmania. It has a powerful bite and hunts other animals.

Frilled-neck lizard

Budgerigars live in huge flocks in central Australia.

Shrimp

SOUTHEAST ASIA

Arafura Sea

Spirit house, where people go to worship

Cockatiel

Daly

NORTHERN TERRITORY

The didgeridoo is a traditional Australian wind instrument.

GREAT SANDY DESERT

Uluru (Ayers Rock) is a huge rock formation. It glows red at sunrise and sunset.

SOUTH AUSTRALIA

Flying doctor

GREAT VICTORIA DESERT

Little penguins are the smallest penguins, only 30cm (12in) tall.

Great Australian Bight

Dwarf minke whale

Pearl oyster

Fitzroy

WESTERN AUSTRALIA

Fortescue

Numbat

AUSTRALIA

Red kangaroo

A baby kangaroo is called a joey.

Lupin flowers are grown for their oil and seeds.

Bilby

Australian rules football is a cross between rugby and football or soccer.

Stingrays have deadly stings on their tails.

Native Australians are known as Aboriginals. There are over 400 different Aboriginal groups.

INDIAN OCEAN

EQUATOR

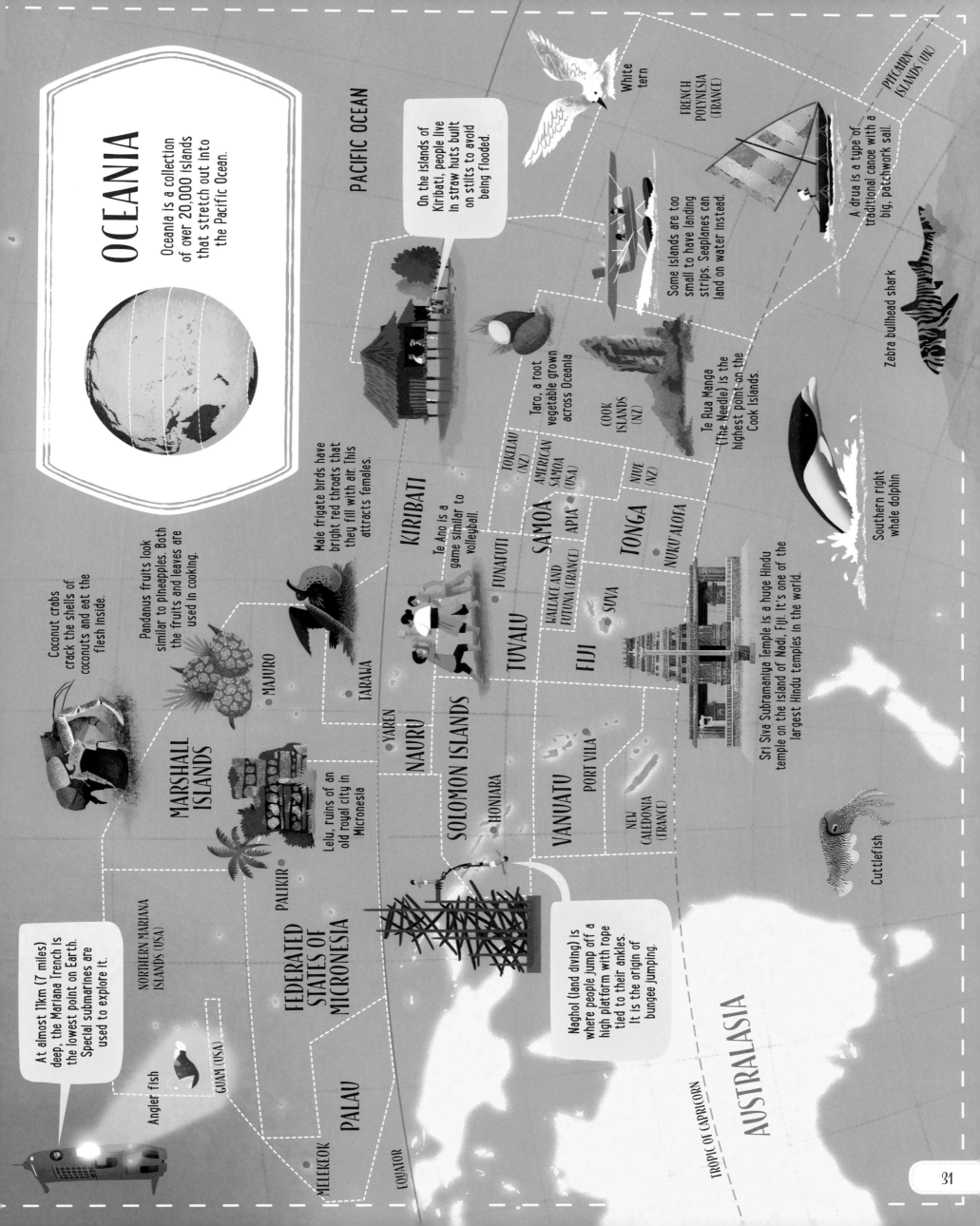

OCEANIA

Oceania is a collection of over 20,000 islands that stretch out into the Pacific Ocean.

PACIFIC OCEAN

On the islands of Kiribati, people live in straw huts built on stilts to avoid being flooded.

White tern

FRENCH POLYNESIA (FRANCE)

PITCAIRN ISLANDS (UK)

A drua is a type of traditional canoe with a big, patchwork sail.

Some islands are too small to have landing strips. Seaplanes can land on water instead.

Zebra bullhead shark

Taro, a root vegetable grown across Oceania

COOK ISLANDS (NZ)

Te Rua Manga (The Needle) is the highest point on the Cook Islands.

Southern right whale dolphin

Male frigate birds have bright red throats that they fill with air. This attracts females.

KIRIBATI

Te Ano is a game similar to volleyball.

TOKELAU (NZ)

AMERICAN SAMOA (USA)

SAMOA
• APIA

NIUE (NZ)

TONGA
• NUKU'ALOFA

FUNAFUTI •

WALLACE AND FUTUNA (FRANCE)

TUVALU

FIJI
• SUVA

Sri Siva Subramaniya Temple is a huge Hindu temple on the island of Nadi, Fiji. It's one of the largest Hindu temples in the world.

Pandanus fruits look similar to pineapples. Both the fruits and leaves are used in cooking.

• MAJURO

• TARAWA

• YAREN
NAURU

SOLOMON ISLANDS

• HONIARA

VANUATU
• PORT VILA

NEW CALEDONIA (FRANCE)

Cuttlefish

Coconut crabs crack the shells of coconuts and eat the flesh inside.

MARSHALL ISLANDS

Lelu, ruins of an old royal city in Micronesia

PALIKIR •

FEDERATED STATES OF MICRONESIA

Naghol (land diving) is where people jump off a high platform with rope tied to their ankles. It is the origin of bungee jumping.

At almost 11km (7 miles) deep, the Mariana Trench is the lowest point on Earth. Special submarines are used to explore it.

Angler fish

NORTHERN MARIANA ISLANDS (USA)

GUAM (USA)

MELEKEOK

PALAU

EQUATOR

TROPIC OF CAPRICORN

AUSTRALASIA

THE ARCTIC

Yupik people live in Alaska and the far east of Russia. They live by hunting and fishing, and build underground houses to keep warm.

Chukchi people live in eastern Russia. This is a Chukchi family wearing traditional dress, including reindeer fur coats.

PACIFIC OCEAN

Bering Sea

Yupik people do dances to tell stories.

Some Yupik dancers wear carved wooden masks, like this one.

A male hooded seal attracts a female by inflating part of its nose.

ARCTIC CIRCLE

ALASKA (USA)

Ivory gull

Chukchi Sea

WRANGEL ISLAND

Kolyma

Horned puffin

East Siberian Sea

Arctic tern

NEW SIBERIAN ISLANDS

Saxifrage

Lena

Beaufort Sea

King crabs have large bodies and long legs. They're a delicacy, and are caught by crab fishermen.

There isn't any land at the North Pole, and there isn't actually a pole there either, just a thick layer of ice.

Laptev Sea

RUSSIA

CANADA

Arctic poppies

Only a few plants grow in the Arctic during summer, when the ice starts to melt.

White cottongrass

ELLESMERE ISLAND

NORTH POLE

Lemming

SEVERNAYA ZEMLYA

Hudson Bay

ARCTIC OCEAN

Arctic wolf

Arctic explorer camping on the ice

Kara Sea

FRANZ JOSEF LAND

BAFFIN ISLAND

Greenland Sea

GREENLAND

NOVAYA ZEMLYA

Nurd Kamal in Norilsk is one of the most northerly mosques in the world.

SVALBARD (NORWAY)

It's so cold here, houses and even whole hotels have been made from blocks of ice.

Fishing village

Research boat

Barents Sea

Ice hotel

Many people on Greenland make their living by fishing.

NORWAY

SWEDEN

FINLAND

ICELAND

Narwhal have long tusks, which can grow to half the length of their bodies.

ATLANTIC OCEAN

32

ATLANTIC OCEAN

Blue whales are the largest animals on Earth. They can grow to 30m (98ft) – longer than a tennis court.

Icefish have special blood that keeps flowing even in freezing cold water.

The only people who live in Antarctica are scientists from many different countries. They come to study the wildlife, ice and environment.

ANTARCTIC CIRCLE

Antarctic pearlwort

Weddell Sea

Weddell seals

ANTARCTIC PENINSULA

RONNE ICE SHELF

VINSON MASSIF

Land in Antarctica is covered in layers of ice that have been forming for thousands of years. Scientists drill into the ice to find out what the surface was like a long time ago.

Scientist releasing a weather balloon to measure temperature, wind speeds and air pressure

Antarctica is the coldest place in the world. Temperatures can drop to below -60°C (-79°F).

Scientists live and work in a research building called the Amundsen-Scott Station.

Emperor penguins lay eggs and raise their chicks during the freezing Antarctic winter.

SOUTH POLE

Snow petrel

ELLSWORTH MOUNTAINS

TRANSANTARCTIC MOUNTAINS

Polar explorer

Leopard seals hunt penguins.

Adélie penguins

ROSS ICE SHELF

Emperor penguins can grow to over 1m (3½ft) tall. They're the largest type of penguin.

Elephant seal

Ross Sea

Krill

Gentoo penguins

SOUTHERN OCEAN

Penguins and whales eat krill, which are similar to small shrimp.

Icebergs are huge, floating blocks of ice. Only the tip floats above the water.

Wandering albatross

ANTARCTICA

Colossal squid

33

FLAGS OF THE WORLD

There are just under 200 countries in the world. Their flags are shown on the next few pages, with their capitals underneath (some countries have more than one capital).

Europe (west)
PAGES 6–7

ANDORRA
Andorra la Vella

AUSTRIA
Vienna

BELGIUM
Brussels

CROATIA
Zagreb

CZECH REPUBLIC
Prague

DENMARK
Copenhagen

FINLAND
Helsinki

FRANCE
Paris

GERMANY
Berlin

ICELAND
Reykjavik

IRELAND
Dublin

ITALY
Rome

LIECHTENSTEIN
Vaduz

LUXEMBOURG
Luxembourg

MALTA
Valletta

MONACO

NETHERLANDS
Amsterdam,
The Hague

NORWAY
Oslo

PORTUGAL
Lisbon

SAN MARINO
San Marino

SLOVENIA
Lubljana

SPAIN
Madrid

SWEDEN
Stockholm

SWITZERLAND
Bern

UNITED KINGDOM
London

VATICAN CITY

Europe (continued) & Russia
PAGES 8–11

ALBANIA
Tirana

BELARUS
Minsk

BOSNIA AND HERZEGOVINA
Sarajevo

BULGARIA
Sofia

CYPRUS
Nicosia

ESTONIA
Tallinn

GREECE
Athens

HUNGARY
Budapest

KOSOVO
Pristina

LATVIA
Riga

LITHUANIA
Vilnius

MACEDONIA
Skopje

MOLDOVA
Chişinău

MONTENEGRO
Podgorica

POLAND
Warsaw

ROMANIA
Bucharest

RUSSIA
Moscow

SERBIA
Belgrade

SLOVAKIA
Bratislava

TURKEY
Ankara

UKRAINE
Kiev

Western & central Asia
→ PAGES 12-13

AFGHANISTAN
Kabul

ARMENIA
Yerevan

AZERBAIJAN
Baku

BAHRAIN
Manama

GEORGIA
Tbilisi

IRAN
Tehran

IRAQ
Baghdad

ISRAEL
Jerusalem

JORDAN
Amman

KAZAKHSTAN
Astana

KUWAIT
Kuwait City

KYRGYSTAN
Bishkek

LEBANON
Beirut

OMAN
Muscat

QATAR
Doha

SAUDI ARABIA
Riyadh

SYRIA
Damascus

TAJIKISTAN
Dushanbe

TURKEY
Ankara

TURKMENISTAN
Ashgabat

UNITED ARAB EMIRATES
Abu Dhabi

UZBEKISTAN
Tashkent

YEMEN
Sana'a

Southern Asia
PAGES 14-15

BANGLADESH
Dhaka

BHUTAN
Thimphu

BURMA (MYANMAR)
Naypyidaw, Rangoon

INDIA
New Delhi

THE MALDIVES
Malé

NEPAL
Kathmandu

PAKISTAN
Islamabad

SRI LANKA
Colombo,
Sri Jayawardenepura Kotte

Eastern Asia
→
PAGES 16-17

CHINA
Beijing

JAPAN
Tokyo

MONGOLIA
Ulan Bator

NORTH KOREA
Pyongyang

SOUTH KOREA
Seoul

Southeast Asia
★ PAGES 18-19 ★

BRUNEI
Bandar Seri Begawan

CAMBODIA
Phnom Penh

EAST TIMOR
Dili

INDONESIA
Jakarta

LAOS
Vientiane

MALAYSIA
Kuala Lumpur,
Putrajaya

PHILIPPINES
Manila

SINGAPORE
Singapore

THAILAND
Bangkok

VIETNAM
Hanoi

Northern Africa
PAGES 20-21

ALGERIA
Algiers

BENIN
Porto-Novo

BURKINA FASO
Ouagadougou

CAMEROON
Yaoundé

CAPE VERDE
Praia

CENTRAL AFRICAN REPUBLIC
Bangui

CHAD
N'Djamena

DJIBOUTI
Djibouti

EGYPT
Cairo

EQUATORIAL GUINEA
Malabo

ERITREA
Asmara

ETHIOPIA
Addis Ababa

THE GAMBIA
Banjul

GHANA
Accra

GUINEA
Conakry

GUINEA-BISSAU
Bissau

IVORY COAST
Yamoussoukro

LIBERIA
Monrovia

LIBYA
Tripoli

MALI
Bamako

MAURITANIA
Nouakchott

MOROCCO
Rabat

NIGER
Niamey

NIGERIA
Abuja

SENEGAL
Dakar

SIERRA LEONE
Freetown

SOMALIA
Mogadishu

SOUTH SUDAN
Juba

SUDAN
Khartoum

TOGO
Lomé

TUNISIA
Tunis

Southern Africa
PAGES 22-23

ANGOLA
Luanda

BOTSWANA
Gabarone

BURUNDI
Bujumbura

COMOROS
Moroni

CONGO
Brazzaville

DEMOCRATIC REPUBLIC OF THE CONGO
Kinshasa

GABON
Libreville

KENYA
Nairobi

LESOTHO
Maseru

MADAGASCAR
Antananarivo

MALAWI
Lilongwe

MAURITIUS
Port Louis

MOZAMBIQUE
Maputo

NAMIBIA
Windhoek

RWANDA
Kigali

SÃO TOMÉ AND PRÍNCIPE
São Tomé

SEYCHELLES
Victoria

SOUTH AFRICA
Pretoria, Cape Town, Bloemfontein

SWAZILAND
Lobamba, Mbabane

TANZANIA
Dodoma, Dar es Salaam

UGANDA
Kampala

ZAMBIA
Lusaka

ZIMBABWE
Harare

USA & CANADA
PAGES 24-25

USA
Washington, D.C.

CANADA
Ottawa

Central America & The Caribbean
PAGES 26-27

ANTIGUA AND BARBUDA
St. John's

THE BAHAMAS
Nassau

BARBADOS
Bridgetown

BELIZE
Belmopan

COSTA RICA
San José

CUBA
Havana

DOMINICA
Roseau

DOMINICAN REPUBLIC
Santo Domingo

EL SALVADOR
San Salvador

GRENADA
St. George's

GUATEMALA
Guatemala City

HAITI
Port-au-Prince

HONDURAS
Tegucigalpa

JAMAICA
Kingston

MEXICO
Mexico City

NICARAGUA
Managua

PANAMA
Panama City

ST. KITTS AND NEVIS
Basseterre

ST. LUCIA
Castries

ST. VINCENT AND THE GRENADINES
Kingstown

TRINIDAD AND TOBAGO
Port-of-Spain

South America
PAGES 28-29

ARGENTINA
Buenos Aires

BOLIVIA
Sucre, Le Paz

BRAZIL
Brasilia

CHILE
Santiago

COLOMBIA
Bogotá

ECUADOR
Quito

GUYANA
Georgetown

PARAGUAY
Asunción

PERU
Lima

SURINAME
Paramaribo

URUGUAY
Montevideo

VENEZUELA
Caracas

Australasia
PAGE 30

AUSTRALIA
Canberra

NEW ZEALAND
Wellington

PAPUA NEW GUINEA
Port Moresby

Oceania
PAGE 31

FIJI
Suva

KIRIBATI
Tarawa

MARSHALL ISLANDS
Majuro

FEDERATED STATES OF MICRONESIA
Palikir

NAURU
Yaren

PALAU
Melekeok

SAMOA
Apia

SOLOMON ISLANDS
Honiara

TONGA
Nuku'alofa

TUVALU
Funufuti

VANUATU
Port Vila

INDEX

MANAGING DESIGNER *Zoe Wray* MANAGING EDITOR *Ruth Brocklehurst*
DIGITAL MANIPULATION *John Russell* MAP CONSULTANT *Craig Asquith*

Additional illustration by Zoe Wray and Emily Barden

First published in 2016 by Usborne Publishing Ltd., Usborne House, 83–85 Saffron Hill, London, EC1N 8RT, England.
www.usborne.com Copyright © 2016 Usborne Publishing Ltd. All rights reserved. No part of this publication may be reproduced, stored in a retrieval system or transmitted in any form or by any means, electronic, mechanical, photocopying, recording or otherwise, without the prior permission of the publisher. The name Usborne and the devices ♀⊕ are Trade Marks of Usborne Publishing Ltd. UE. First published in America 2016.